Quick Handlebar Templ

I0004623

Published By
Sandeep Kumar Patel.

Table of Contents

Contents

Chapter 1 Introduction to Handlebar

In this chapter, you will learn about the need of a templating library for a web application development followed by a quick introduction to Handlebar.

Why Templating?

In present era, Most of the web applications are based on AJAX technology. Browser and server communication are more frequent and asynchronous in nature. Typical scenarios in all web application are as follows:-

-Server sends response data in JSON format.

-Browser prepares and renders the HTML markup using JSON data and JavaScript or Jquery code.

Above steps results in more code and requires more effort in maintaining the code. We need an approach where we can separate our HTML markup and logic code to overcome the above issue. This is where templating comes in picture. It helps the developer to produce reusable code with a proper separation of markup and logic.

What is Templating?

Below diagram shows the building blocks of a templating framework. There are mainly four different entities in the process.

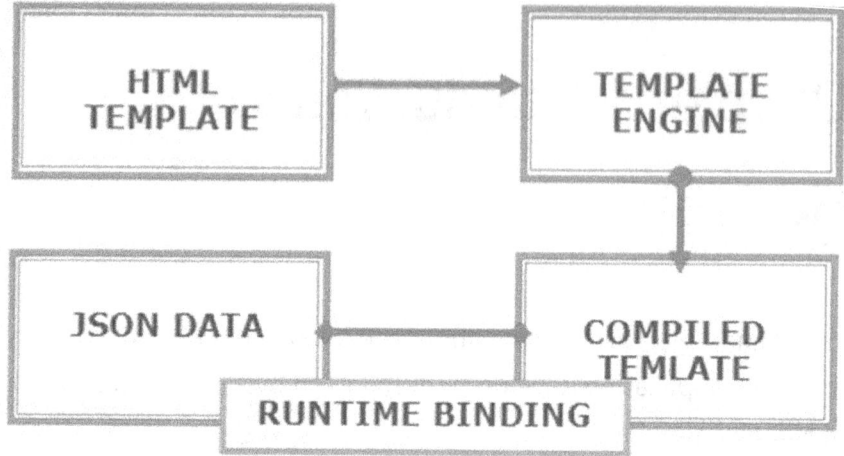

Building Blocks of a Templating Framework

A templating framework follows the below steps:-

-A HTML template is prepared by the developer.

-HTML template can be compiled in the server side or client side to produce the compiled version of the template. The compiled code is nothing other than JavaScript.

-At the runtime browser will do the binding between the JSON data and compiled template to produce the HTML markup code for rendering.

Handlebar Templating

Handlebar library is based on logic less templating framework. Logic less templates is purely for rendering purpose without doing any operation on the JSON data. It is almost similar to **"Fill in the blank"** type exercised, where we need to put our answers to complete the statement. Compiled handlebar templates provide placeholders to fill up by the browser at runtime to produce the meaningful HTML markup for rendering.

Handlebar has a built-in compiler in JavaScript. This compiler takes handlebar expressions as an input produces the compiled code as a JavaScript function. This JavaScript function takes a single argument as JSON object to produce the HTML code.

Benefits of Handlebar

Below points are some of the benefits by using the handlebar library:-

-Handlebar is logic less, this helps in creating separation of concern for views.

-Reusability of code is increased as there is no depended logical code inside the template.

-Maintenance is easier and straight forward as there is no spaghetti code present inside the markup.

-Huge Developer community base is present for help.

Handlebar Features

Some of the important features provided by handlebars are:-

Expressions: are used to create a template using HTML markup.

Comments: are used for providing comments inside the template markup.

Relative Path: are used to access value of the object from a different context.

Built-in Helpers: are used to create template base on condition, iteration and etc.

Custom Helpers: are used to create additional helpers for use in template.

Partials: are sub templates.

In the upcoming chapters we will explore these features with more details with coding examples.

Conclusion

In this chapter we have learnt about the benefits and working flow of a templating framework followed by a quick introduction to handlebar library.

Chapter 2 Configuring Application

In this Chapter We will follow step by step method to setup the demo application for handlebar library demonstration.

Step 1 Creating Directory Structure

Handlebar templates can be configured in server or client side. With a server side configuration handlebar templates can be pre compiled during the build time. Server sends both JSON data and pre compiled templates to the browser for rendering purpose. It increases the client side performance.

However this book is only deals with handlebar configuration in client side. In this chapter we will explore client side compilation of templates.Handlebar library can be downloaded from http://handlebarsjs.com web page. This is the home site for handlebar library. The library code present **handlebar.js** file. Below is the directory structure of our demo project,

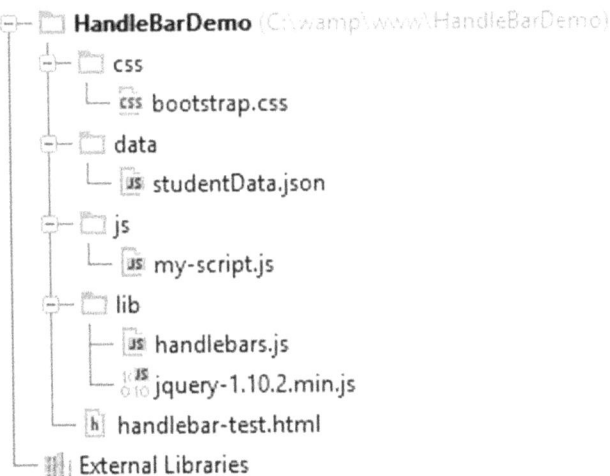

Project Structure

The details of the above directory structures are as below:-

css: This directory has the bootstrap styles in **bootstrap.css** file.

data: This directory has static student data packaged in **studentData.json** file.

js: This directory has the JavaScript file **my-script.js,** code related to the demo.

lib: It contains all the JavaScript library files **handlebars.js** and **Jquery-1.10.2.min.js.**

Step 2 Calling Handlebar Library

Handlebar library called using the script tag and pointing src attribute to the file. The syntax is as follows:

```
<script src="lib/handlebars.js"></script>
```

In our demo application **handlebar-test.html** file contains the code for calling the handlebar library.

```html
<! DOCTYPE html>
<html>
<head>
    <title>HandleBar Templating Framework</title>
    <link rel="stylesheet" href="css/bootstrap.css">
</head>
    <body>
      <div id="my-container">
      </div>
    <!--Handlebar template library call-->
    <script src="lib/jquery-1.10.2.min.js"></script>
    <script src="lib/handlebars.js"></script>
    <script src="js/my-script.js"></script>
    </body>
</html>
```
handlebar-test.html

Step 3 Packaging Static JSON Data

In this step we will create some Student data and package them in JSON file **studentData.json**. We will use this static data throughout this book to explore different features handlebar framework.

```
{"course":"M.Tech Computer",
  "coursedetail":{"type":"Post Graduation",
      "duration":2,
      "semester":{"no":"2nd Sem", "semtype":"year end"}
    },"students": [ {"name": "sandeep",
```

```json
            "mark": 35,
            "subject": "Geography",
            "parent":{"father":"Dilip Patel",
"mother":"Sanjukta Patel"},
            "hobbies": ["cricket" , "football"]
        }, { "name": " Jack ",
            "subject": "English",
            "address":"Chennai,India",
            "parent":{"father":"Mr JKL OPQ", "mother":"Mr.
EFG  HIJ"},
            "hobbies": []
        }, { "name": "John",
            "mark": 55,
            "subject": "English",
            "parent":{"father":"Mr. ABCD EFGH",
"mother":"Mrs. XYZA BCDE"},
            "hobbies": ["tennis" , "football"]
}]}
```
studentData.json

Conclusion

In this chapter we have done the setup for an application to use in our upcoming chapter for demonstration of handlebar features.

Chapter 3 Quick Start with Handlebar

In this chapter we will create a quick handlebar template and will be introduced to client side compilation of the template.

Example of Handlebar Template

In Chapter 2 we have created static JSON data about the student detail in the file **studentData.json**. The whole application directory is copied to a local **WAMP** server **www** directory hosted in default port 80.This object has two parent field **course** and **students**. In this section we will create a handlebar template to print the course name on the browser.

Follow the below steps to create a sample handlebar template:-

Step 1 creating the template

A handlebar template is similar to a HTML document with handlebar expression.

-Handlebar expressions are the placeholders for the real data.

-A handlebar expression is wrapped inside the "{{ }}" brackets.

-For displaying course name in the browser the template will look be like below,

```
| <h3> {{course}} </h3>
```

Step 2 delivering the template-

-To deliver the prepared template to the browser we need to wrap this code inside a script tag.

-Syntax,"**<script id=" XXXX" type="text/x-handlebars-template">...</script>**".

-Wrapped template for the course will look like below,

```
<script id="course-template" type="text/x-handlebars-template">
    <h3> {{ course }}</h3>
</script>
```

Steps 3 compiling the template

-Template can be compiled both in the server and client side.

- If you are compiling the template in server side and delivering it to browser then there is no need to use **Handlbar.js** file instead of that use **handlebars.runtime.js** which has a small footprint.

-However In this book we will compile our code in the client side.

-**Handlebar.js** file comes with a packaged template compiler.

-Syntax, **" Handlebars. compile (<templatestring>)"**.

-Compile function takes a string as argument and return a JavaScript function. This returned function is our compiled code. To compile the code for course template use the below code,

```
var templateSource   = $("#student-template").html(),
        compiledTemplate =
    Handlebars.compile(templateSource);
```

Steps 4 producing the markup

-The required HTML markup can be produced by passing the JSON object to the compiled template (JavaScript function).

-The JavaScript code will be as below,

```
var courseHTML = compiledTemplate(resJSON);
```

Step 5 rendering in browser

-The produced HTML markup can be rendered by appending to a DOM element.

-In our Example we are going to replace the inner HTML of a container. The code will look like below,

```
$('#my-container').html (courseHTML);
```

Above steps are present below in two files **handlebar-test.html** and **my-script.js** respectively.

```html
<!DOCTYPE html>
<html>
<head>
    <title>HandleBar Quick Example</title>
    <link rel="stylesheet" href="css/bootstrap.css">
</head>
    <body>
        <div id="my-container">
        </div>
        <!--Handlebar templates start-->
        <script id="course-template" type="text/x-handlebars-template">
            <h3>{{ course }}</h3>
        </script>
        <!--Handlebar templates end-->
        <script src="lib/jquery-1.10.2.min.js"></script>
        <script src="lib/handlebars.js"></script>
        <script src="js/my-script.js"></script>
    </body>
</html>
```

handlebar-test.html

```javascript
var STUDENT_METHOD = {
    /*Handler for success event of AJAX call*/
    handlerData: function (resJSON) {
        var templateSource = $("#course-template").html(),
            compiledTemplate =
Handlebars.compile(templateSource),
            courseHTML = compiledTemplate(resJSON);
        $('#my-container').html(courseHTML);
    },
    /*JQUERY AJAX method to laod the student JSON data*/
    loadCourseName: function () {
        $.ajax({
            url:
"http://localhost/HandleBarDemo/data/studentData.json",
            method: 'get',
            success: this.handlerData
        })}
};
$(document).ready(function () {
    STUDENT_METHOD.loadCourseName();
});
```

my-script.js

The output of the above example will look like below screenshot. The output is "M.Tech Computer" and the Firebug console is showing the AJAX call.

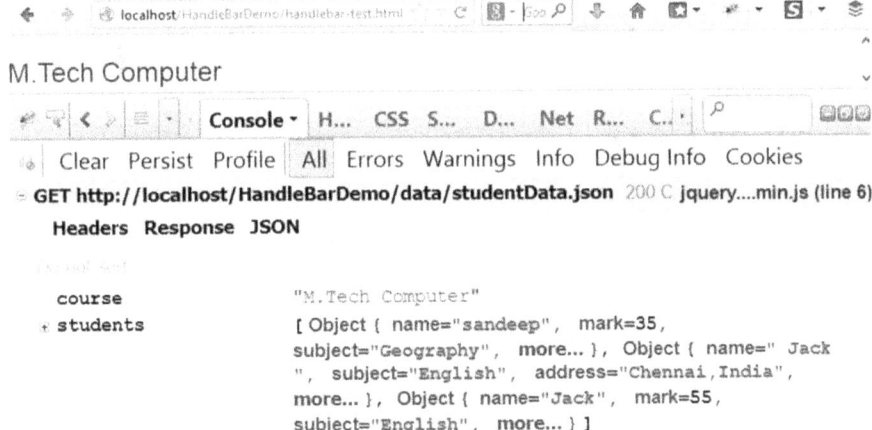

course   "M.Tech Computer"

+ students   [Object { name="sandeep", mark=35,
                subject="Geography", more... }, Object { name=" Jack
                ", subject="English", address="Chennai,India",
                more... }, Object { name="Jack", mark=55,
                subject="English", more... }]

Output in Firefox Browser

Conclusion

In this section we have introduced with a handlebar template example. We have understood the steps to be follow while working with handlebar template.

Chapter 4 Expressions, Path and Comments

In this chapter we will learn about handlebar expression, use of relative path and comments.

Handlebar Expressions

Expressions in handlebar are like placeholder where the real value will be bind in runtime to produce HTML markup. A handlebar expression is represented by '{{}}' braces wrapped around an object.

We have seen in the previous chapter, {{**course**}} used to print the course name. It is an example of handlebar expression.

Triple Stash Expression

This expression is represented by '{{{ }}}' braces. This is used to prevent the escaping HTML by the handlebar expression. By default, handlebar expression escapes HTML markup present in the data.

Example

-Suppose the **course** field in JSON data has HTML markup inside wrapped around look like below,

```
{
    "course":"<i>M.Tech Computer</i>",
    .............
}
```

-Let the handlebar template has both normal and triple stash expression like below,

```
<script id="course-template" type="text/x-handlebars-template">
    <h3>{{ course }}</h3>
```

```
    <h3>{{{ course }}}</h3>
</script>
```

-The HTML markup will be rendered in the browser like below,

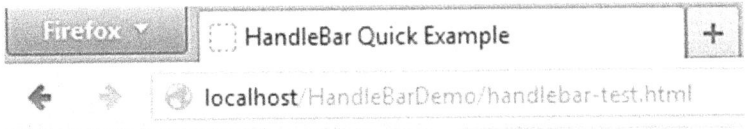

\<i\>M.Tech Computer\</i\>

M.Tech Computer

Dot Operator

Handlebar expression supports dot operator to access inner property of a JSON object. The syntax for using dot operator is "{{<objectName>.<propertyName>}}".

Example

-Inside the JSON data we have a **'semester'** object with 2

properties **'no'** and **'semtype'** with some value as below,

```
{
    ...............;
    "coursedetail":{
        "type":"Post Graduation",
        "duration":2,
        "semester":{"no":"2nd Sem", "semtype":"year end"}
    },
    "students": [
        ...........
    ]
}
```

-To access the value of **'no'** and **'semtype'** we have to use

{{coursedetail.semester.no}} and

{{coursedetail.semester.semtype}}. The handlebar template will

look like below,

```
<script id="course-template" type="text/x-handlebars-
template">
    <h3>{{ coursedetail.semester.no }}</h3>
    <h3>{{ coursedetail.semester.semtype }}</h3>
</script>
```

-The generated markup for above template will render in the browser as below,

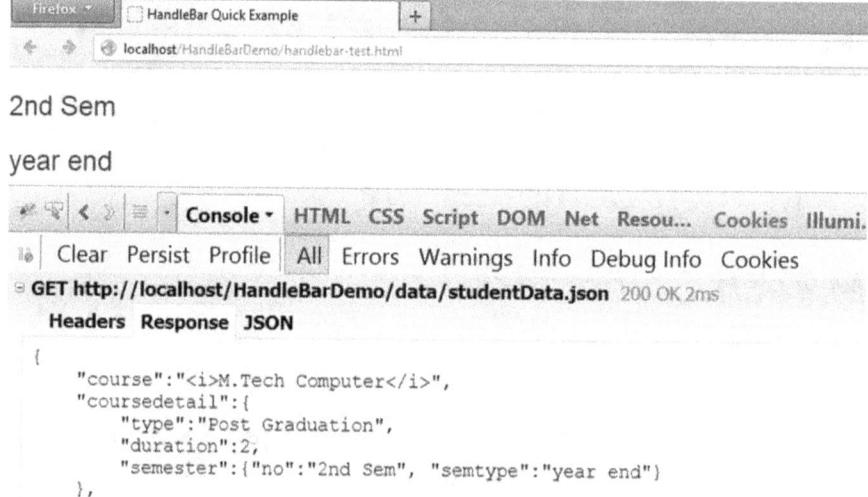

2nd Sem

year end

Path

Handlebar supports property value access using path .It is almost similar to a dot operator. The difference only comes with power of using relative path notation. A path is represented by a forward slash **"/"** notation.

The syntax for a simple path is

{{<objectname>/<propertyname>}}.

Example

-Template example given for the dot operator to access 'no' and 'semtype' property from the **'coursedetail'** object is can be converted into path notation as below,

```
<script id="course-template" type="text/x-handlebars-template">
    <h3>{{ coursedetail/semester/no }}</h3>
    <h3>{{ coursedetail/semester/semtype }}</h3>
</script>
```

Relative path feature provides access to object which are not in the current context. Notation for relative path are '**./**' represents current context and '**../**' represents parent's context. It is useful while iterating an object array and if there is a need to access some other object which is not in the context. We will see am example in the next chapter when I will demonstrate about built-in helpers.

Comment

Comments are very useful feature for all the languages and helps in documenting the code. It can be used inside a handlebar template and it is ignored by the compiler hence it is not present in the generated markup.

In handlebar comment can be done using two syntaxes {{! }} or {{!----}}.

Example,

Let's comment in our template .It will look like below code,

```
<script id="course-template" type="text/x-handlebars-template">
    {{!For accessing no property of semester object from coursedetail }}
        <h3>{{ coursedetail.semester.no }}</h3>
    {{!--For accessing no property of semester object from coursedetail--}}
        <h3>{{ coursedetail.semester.semtype }}</h3>
</script>
```

Conclusion

In this chapter we have learnt:-

-About expressions used as placeholder.

-How to access a nested property.

-Use of path notation.

-Use of comments inside a template.

Chapter 5 Built-In Helpers

In this chapter, we will explore available built-in helpers in handlebar library wand there use in authoring a template.

Block Helpers

These helpers are useful for managing different block of markup. Helpers are useful for conditional based markup generation and leads to less code. Some of the useful block helpers are listed below.

Helpers	Type
If	Condition based markup generation.
If..Else	Condition based alternate markup generation.
Unless	Condition based markup generation with falsy value
Each	Iteration and Condition based markup generation.
With	Context based markup generation.

List of Built-In Helpers

If And If...Else Helper

Some points about these helpers are listed below:-

-Both the helpers are useful for conditional block of markup generation. Syntax for using 'If' helper inside a template is {{#if <truth-value>}}... {{/if}}.Code inside the block will not execute for a false truth values.

-Syntax for using 'If...Else' helper inside a template is {{#if <truth-value>}}...{{/else}}...{{/if}}. In 'If...Else' helper 2 block of code are take participation on rendering the markup. Either of the blocks gets qualified based on the truth value. The else part represents the falsy value.

-Handlebar considers **false, undefined, null, ""** and [ ] are falsy.

Example,

Below code shows a template accessing **coursedetail.semester.no** and **coursedetail.semester.fee** from the JSON data. You can see 'no' property is present inside the **cousedetail** object however there is no 'fee' property.

-The JSON data will look like below,

```
{
    "course":"<i>M.Tech Computer</i>",
    "coursedetail":{
        "type":"Post Graduation",
        "duration":2,
        "semester":{"no":"2nd Sem", "semtype":"year end"}
    },
    "students": [
        .........]}
```

-Below code shows the use of 'If' and 'If...Else' in below template.

The first block is a single if block checking for 'no' property exists then prints some message. The second block 'If...Else' checks the existence of 'fee' property and have two block of template for the truth values.

```
<script id="course-template" type="text/x-handlebars-template">
    {{#if coursedetail.semester.no }}
        <h4> Course Duration is {{coursedetail.semester.no }}</h4>
    {{/if}}
    {{#if coursedetail.semester.fee }}
        <h4> Course Fee is {{coursedetail.semester.fee }}</h4>
    {{else}}
        <h4> Course Fee is not present.</h4>
    {{/if}}
</script>
```

-Output of the above template looks like below

Course Duration is 2nd Sem

Course Fee is not present.

Console ▾ HTML CSS Script DOM Net Resou... Cookies Illum

Clear Persist Profile | All | Errors Warnings Info Debug Info Cookies

GET http://localhost/HandleBarDemo/data/studentData.json 200 OK 2ms

Headers Response JSON

```
{
    "course":"<i>M.Tech Computer</i>",
    "coursedetail":{
        "type":"Post Graduation",
        "duration":2,
        "semester":{"no":"2nd Sem", "semtype":"year end"}
    },
    "students": [
```

Unless Helper

Some points on unless helpers are listed below:-

- 'Unless' is similar to 'If' helper except it operate on the 'falsy' value.

-The block of template gets executed if a false value is passed to 'Unless'.

Example,

If property 'fee' is present or not. But you can see there is no property name **'fee'** present inside the **'coursedetail'** property.

-Below code is showing the use of **'unless'** helper use,

```
<script id="course-template" type="text/x-handlebars-template">
  {{#unless coursedetail.semester.fee }}
    <h4> Course Fee is not present.</h4>
  {{/unless}}
</script>
```

-Output of the above code renders as below on the Firefox browser,

Course Fee is not present.

GET http://localhost/HandleBarDemo/data/studentData.json 200 OK 195ms

Headers Response JSON

```
{
    "course":"<i>M.Tech Computer</i>",
    "coursedetail":{
        "type":"Post Graduation",
        "duration":2,
        "semester":{"no":"2nd Sem", "semtype":"year end"}
    },
```

With Helper

Some points about 'With' helper are listed below:-

- **'With'** is a contextual based helper.

- It checks for the current context for the given data and generated the markup for it.

- It is relay helpful for context switching inside the JSON data.

Example,
'coursedetail' has three properties **'type','duration'** and **'semester'**.It means all these three properties shares a single context.

- Below code is showing the contextual based property access from **'coursedetail'**.It also have a nested **'with'** helper that has 2 properties **'no'** and **'semtype'** sharing a single context.

```
<script id="course-template" type="text/x-handlebars-
template">
    {{#with coursedetail}}
        <h4>Type of Course :- {{type}}</h4>
        <h4>Duration of Course :- {{duration}}</h4>
        {{#with semester}}
            <h4>Number of Course :- {{no}}</h4>
            <h4>Semester type :- {{semtype}}</h4>
        {{/with}}
    {{/with}}
</script>
```

-The output of the above template render as below in browser.

localhost/HandleBarDemo/handlebar-test.html

Type of Course :- Post Graduation

Duration of Course :- 2

Number of Course :- 2nd Sem

Semester type :- year end

Console ▾ HTML CSS Script DOM Net Resou

Clear Persist Profile All Errors Warnings Info Debug I

GET http://localhost/HandleBarDemo/data/studentData.json 200 O

Headers Response JSON

```
{
    "course":"<i>M.Tech Computer</i>",
    "coursedetail":{
        "type":"Post Graduation",
        "duration":2,
        "semester":{"no":"2nd Sem", "semtype":"year end"}
    },
```

Each Helper

Some points about 'Each' helper are listed below:-

- **'Each'** helper is used for iteration over a list.

- Every iteration is a context based.

- It also provides indexing for each iteration through **{{@index}}** notation.

Example

In the JSON data **'students'** property is having an array of student object.Every student object has some property in common.

-Below code shows the use of **'Each'** helper .It iterates over the student objects and print there name with their index position inside the list.

```
<script id="course-template" type="text/x-handlebars-
template">
```

```
    <h4>Name Of the students are :</h4>
    <ol>
        {{#each students}}
            <li>{{name}} with index : {{@index}}</li>
        {{/each}}
    </ol>
</script>
```

-The generated markup using the above template and the JSON

data will render like below screenshot,

Name Of the students are :

1. sandeep with index : o

2. Jack with index : 1

3. John with index : 2

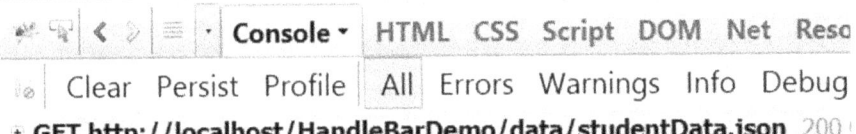

Conclusion

In this chaper we have seen built-helpers and their use inside a
template.

Chapter 6 Custom Helpers

In This Chapter We will follow some steps to create a user defined helper and use it in our template.

Student Table Template

Before going into the steps for creating custom helpers lets create handlebar template to render the student data as table.We will use this table and template as a base of our next section on creating custom helper.

-For this let's use the **studentData.json** file as input and

bootstrap.css for styling the table. Below code shows the template for student table:-

```html
<!--Handlebar Student templates start-->
<script id="student-template" type="text/x-handlebars-template">
    <table class="table table-striped">
        <thead>
        <tr>
            <th>Name</th>
            <th>Mark</th>
            <th>Subject</th>
        </tr>
        </thead>
        <tbody>
        {{#each students}}
        <tr>
            <td>{{ this.name }}</td>
            <td>{{this.mark }}</td>
            <td>{{ this.subject }}</td>
        </tr>
        {{/each}}
        </tbody>
    </table>
</script>
<!--Handlebar Student templates end-->
```

-The below screenshot shows the table produced by using above template and **studentData.json** file.It has three headers **name,mark** and **subject**.

Name	Mark	Subject
sandeep	35	Geography
Jack		English
John	55	English

🔧 🔍 ‹ › ≡ · **Console ▾** HTML CSS Script DOM Net |

🔁 Clear Persist Profile **All** Errors Warnings Info De

⊞ **GET http://localhost/HandleBarDemo/data/studentData.json**

With the base of above template let's create a custom helper **'customMarker'** which will have following functionality:-

-Take the mark of a student and decide whether it is a 'FAIL' or 'PASS'.

-If mark is less then 40 then student is 'FAIL'.

-If mark is more then 40 then student is 'PASS'.

-If no data available about the mark then '-No Data-' will be printed.

Let's checkout all the steps involved to create and use the **'customMarker'** helper.

Step 1 Defining a Custom Helper

HandlebarJS library provides **registerHelper()** method to define a custom helper.Syntax for this method is,

```
Handlebar.registerHelper ("<helper name>", <callback
function (context)>)
```

'context' : Object for which the helper is going to be called.

Code for defining **'customMarker'** is written below,

```
Handlebars.registerHelper("customMarker",
function(studentMark) {
    if(40   < studentMark ){
        return new Handlebars.SafeString(studentMark +"<b
class='pass'> PASS </b>");
    }else if(40 > studentMark){
        return new Handlebars.SafeString(studentMark +"<b
class='fail'> FAIL </b>");
    }else{
        return new Handlebars.SafeString('-No Data-');
    }
});
```

Above code code is explained in below poins:-

-Method **registerHelper()** is having 2 parameters,1ˢᵗ parameter

"customMarker" is the name of the helper.The 2ⁿᵈ paramater is
the callback function on the context object '**studentMark**'
representing mark of the current student.

-The **'If Else'** block is having condition to determine the "**PASS**" or

"**FAIL**" status based on the mark and if no mark is present for a
student then it is returning a string 'No Data'.

-**Handlebars.SafeString()** method is for escaping HTML code

while returning.

Step 2 Using a Custom Helper

Custom Helper can be called with the same syntax like
expression.The syntax for calling the custom helper expression is as
below:-

**{{#<custtom helper name> <contextobject>}}...{{/< custtom
helper name >}}**

For our example 'customMarker' is called as below,

```
<td>{{#customMarker this.mark }}{{/customMarker}}</td>
```
Below code is showing the whole template for the student table

with the use of **'customMarker'** inside the table row,

```
<script id="student-template" type="text/x-handlebars-
template">
    <table class="table table-striped">
        <thead>
        <tr>
            <th>Name</th>
```

```
            <th>Mark</th>
            <th>Subject</th>
        </tr>
        </thead>
        <tbody>
        {{#each students}}
        <tr>
            <td>{{ this.name }}</td>
            <td>
              {{#customMarker this.mark }}
              {{/customMarker}}
            </td>
            <td>{{ this.subject }}</td>
        </tr>
        {{/each}}
        </tbody>
    </table>
</script>
```

- The output of the above code will look like below,

Name	Mark	Subject
sandeep	35 FAIL	Geography
Jack	-No Data-	English
John	55 PASS	English

Console ▾ HTML CSS Script DOM Net Resou... Cookies

Clear Persist Profile All Errors Warnings Info Debug Info Cookies

GET http://localhost/HandleBarDemo/data/studentData.json 200 OK 0ms

Conclusion

In this chapter we have learned the requiered steps to create a custom expression helper in HandlebarJS library.

Chapter 7 Custom Partials

In this chapter we will learn what a partial all is about and how to create custom partial in handlebar library.

Partials

Partials are very useful feature in handlebar library. Generally a block of markup that can be used in different context of object can be made to a partial. It is similar to a utility package. It helps in managing for project where large templates are used.

Defining a Partial

A partial can be defined using **registerPartial()** method . The name of partial and the current context object must have same name. The syntax for declaring a partial is,

> Handlebars.registerPartial(<partial name>, <template or compiled template>)

Calling a Partial

A partial can be called inside a template using '**>**' operator. The Syntax for calling a partial on a object is as below,

> {{> partial-name}}

Example

In previous chapter we have created a custom helper, with the same example let's add another column '**parent**' to show father and mother name with 2 different colors. For this let's create a partial named 'parent' and use it in the table template.

-The template markup for the '**parent**' partial is in below. In JSON data '**parent**' object have 2 property '**father**' and '**mother**'.

```
<script id="parent-partial" type="text/x-handlebars-template">
    <span class="father">{{ parent.father }}</span>-
    <span class="mother">{{ parent.mother }}</span>
</script>
```

-Below code is showing to register a partial,

```
/*CUSTOM PARTIAL : register a new partial 'parent'*/
registerParentPartial : function(){
    Handlebars.registerPartial("parent", $("#parent-
partial").html());
  }
```

-Below code is showing the use of **'parent'** partial in the table

template,

```
<script id="student-template" type="text/x-handlebars-
template">
    <table class="table table-striped">
        <thead>
        <tr>
            <th>Name</th>
            <th>Mark</th>
            <th>Subject</th>
            <th>Parents</th>
        </tr>
        </thead>
        <tbody>
        {{#each students}}
        <tr>
            <td>{{ this.name }}</td>
            <td>
            {{#customMarker this.mark }}
            {{/customMarker}}
            </td>
            <td>{{ this.subject }}</td>
            <td>{{> parent }}</td>
        </tr>
        {{/each}}
        </tbody>
    </table>
</script>
```

-Output of the above code will render as below,

Name	Mark	Subject	Parents
sandeep	35 FAIL	Geography	Dilip Patel-Sanjukta Patel
Jack	-No Data-	English	Mr JKL OPQ-Mr. EFG HIJ
John	55 PASS	English	Mr. ABCD EFGH-Mrs. XYZA BCDE

Console ▾ | HTML CSS Script DOM Net Resou... Cookie

Clear Persist Profile | All | Errors Warnings Info Debug Info Cook

⊕ **GET http://localhost/HandleBarDemo/data/studentData.json** 200 OK 2ms

Conclusion

In this chapter we have learnt to create a partial in handlebar.

Chapter 8 Handlebar Utility Methods

In this chapter we will explore the method present inside the util package of handlebar library.

Util Package

Handlebar library provides some useful methods inside the **"Util"** object. The console log will shows three methods present inside the util object. Check the below screenshot of the util package,

>>> Handlebars.Utils

Three methods are listed below:-

-escapeExpression() :

-isEmpty()

-extend()

Escape Expression

Util package provides **escapeExpression()** method to escape certain special character from a string. Some of the escape characters are ["**&**", "**<**", "**>**","**"**", "**'**","**`**"] and their respective ASCII string representation are [ "**&**", "**<**","**>**","**"**","**'**","**`**"].
Example

Let's create a helper called `escapeExpression` to escape special characters from a string. In the **studentData.json** file there is a `course` property containing HTML tags.

```
{
     "course":"<i>M.Tech Computer</i>",
     "coursedetail":{
          "type":"Post Graduation",
          "duration":2,
          "semester":{"no":"2nd Sem", "semtype":"year end"}
     },
     "students": [
          .........
     ]
}
```

Below code is showing the `escapeExpression` helper definition that takes the context object and process it using **Handlebar.Utils.escapeExpression()** method.

```
Handlebars.registerHelper("escapeExpression",
function(element) {
     return Handlebars.Utils.escapeExpression(element);
})
```

Below HTML template is showing the use of the above `escapeExpression` helper for `course` context.

```
<script id="student-template" type="text/x-handlebars-template">
   <h3>{{ escapeExpression course }}</h3>
</script>
```

Below screen shot showing the output of the above template in the browser with all escape strings are got printed for italic tag.

localhost/HandleBarDemo/handlebar-test.html

<i>M.Tech Computer</i>

			Console ▾	HTML	CSS	Script	DOM	Net	
	Clear	Persist	Profile	All	Errors	Warnings	Info	Del

GET http://localhost/HandleBarDemo/data/studentData.json

Headers Response JSON

```
{
     "course":"<i>M.Tech Computer</i>",
     "coursedetail":{
          "type":"Post Graduation",
```

Is Empty

Util provides **isEmpty()** method to check if a value object is present or not by calculating the length.

Example

Let's create a '**isEmptyCheck**' helper for checking empty condition for the current context.

In '**studentData.json**' file '**course**' property is present with some value but '**course.grade**' is not present.

Below code is showing the '**isEmptyCheck**' helper definition that takes the context object and process it using

Handlebars.Utils.isEmpty() method.

```
Handlebars.registerHelper("isEmptyCheck",
function(element) {
    var isEmpty = Handlebars.Utils.isEmpty(element),
        elementString = element;
    if(isEmpty){
        elementString = " Is Empty.";
    }else{
        elementString += ":- Is Not Empty";
    }
    return elementString;
})
```

Below HTML template is showing the use of the above

'**isEmptyCheck**' helper for '**course**' context.

```
<script id="student-template" type="text/x-handlebars-
template">
    <h3>{{ isEmptyCheck course }}</h3>
    <h3>{{ isEmptyCheck course.grade }}</h3>
</script>
```

Below screen shot is showing the output of the above template in the browser.

M.Tech Computer:- Is Not Empty

Is Empty.

```json
{
    "course":"<i>M.Tech Computer</i>",
    "coursedetail":{
        "type":"Post Graduation",
        "duration":2,
        "semester":{"no":"2nd Sem", "semtype":"year end"}
    },
```

Extending Object

Handlebar util package provides **Handlebars.Utils.extend()** method for extending an object. This is really helpful for extending the util package to add more new utility methods. The syntax for the method is, **Handlebars.Utils.extend(<targetObject>, <sourceObject>)** .All the properties of the **sourceObject** gets copied to **targetObject**.

Example

We will create a new utility method called '**styleRedText'** and it will be accessible using **Handlebars.Utils.styleRedText(text)**.This method takes context string and makes the font color red and bold. Below code is showing a JavaScript function which has the '**styleRedText'** object in name-value pair.Subsequent lines in the code are for extending the **Handlebars.Utils** package for adding this new method.

```javascript
var styleRedText ={"styleRedText":function(element){
    return "<b style='color:red'>"+element+"</b>";
}};
```

```
Handlebars.Utils.extend(Handlebars.Utils, styleRedText);
```
Next we will create a helper **'makeRedFont'** which will use the new
utility method **'styleRedText()'** from the **Handlebars.Utils**
package.
```
Handlebars.registerHelper("makeRedFont", function(element)
{
    return Handlebars.Utils.styleRedText(element);
});
```
Below code is showing the template that uses **'makeRedFont'** on

'course' context from the **StudentData.json** file.
```
<script id="student-template" type="text/x-handlebars-
template">
  <h3>
     {{#makeRedFont course}}
     {{/makeRedFont}}
  </h3>
</script>
```
Output of the above template will render in browser as below,

M.Tech Computer

Console ▾ HTML CSS Script DOM Net Resou

Clear Persist Profile | All | Errors Warnings Info Debug I

GET **http://localhost/HandleBarDemo/data/studentData.json** 200 O

Headers Response JSON

```
{
    "course":"<i>M.Tech Computer</i>",
    "coursedetail":{
        "type":"Post Graduation",
        "duration":2,
        "semester":{"no":"2nd Sem", "semtype":"year end"}
```

Conclusion

In this chapter we have seen utility methods available inside the
handlebar library. We have also learnt to extend object inside
handlebar.

Resources and References

1. Official Site http://handlebarsjs.com .Here you will find all the introduction and documentation of this library.

2. For Online compilation and practice tool http://tryhandlebarsjs.com . This site provides text area for compiling a handlebar template and binding it at runtime to produce HTML markups.

3. My Blog http://www.tutorialsavvy.com/ , some of the posts are handlebar library use.

4. Stack Exchange Developer community for handlebars related question and answers http://stackoverflow.com/questions/tagged/handlebars .

5. Geek developer's community https://geekli.st/community/handlebars .

6. Source code for Handlebar https://github.com/wycats/handlebars.js .

About The Author

Sandeep Kumar Patel is a senior web developer and founder of www.tutorialsavvy.com, a widely- read programming blog since 2012. He has more than four years of experience in object-oriented JavaScript and JSON-based web applications development. He is GATE-2005 Information Technology (IT) qualified and has a Master's degree from VIT University, Vellore.

You can know more about him from his
-LinkedIn profile (http://www.linkedin.com/in/techblogger).
-He has received the Dzone Most Valuable Blogger (MVB) award for technical publications related to web technologies. His article can be viewed at http://www.dzone.com/users/sandeepgiet.
-He has also received the Java Code Geek (JCG) badge for a technical article published in JCG. His article can be viewed at http://www.javacodegeeks.com/author/sandeep-kumar-patel/.
-Author of "Instant GSON" for Packt publication,

http://www.packtpub.com/create-json-data-java-objects-implement-with-gson-library/book

Questions or comments? E-mail me at sandeeppateltech@gmail.com or find me on the following social networks:-
-Facebook Page:

http://www.facebook.com/SandeepTechTutorials .

-Tutorial Blog: http://www.tutorialsavvy.com

One Last Thing...

When you turn the page, Kindle will give you the opportunity to rate this book and share your thoughts on Facebook and Twitter. If you believe the book is worth sharing, please would you take a few seconds to let your friends know about it? If it turns out to make a difference in their professional lives, they'll be forever grateful to you, as will I.

All the best,
Sandeep Kumar Patel.

www.ingramcontent.com/pod-product-compliance
Lightning Source LLC
Chambersburg PA
CBHW060934050326

40689CB00013B/3088